THE STORY OF
NOAH'S ARK

GENESIS 6:5–9:17 FOR CHILDREN

Written by Jane Latourette

Illustrated by Sally Mathews

ARCH® Books

© 1965 CONCORDIA PUBLISHING HOUSE, ST. LOUIS, MISSOURI

LIBRARY OF CONGRESS CATALOG CARD NO. 63-23144
MANUFACTURED IN THE UNITED STATES OF AMERICA
ALL RIGHTS RESERVED
ISBN-0-570-06009-5

The Bible tells that long ago
God looked on earth and here below
saw all His creatures full of hate;
He asked, "Oh, *what* did I create?

"Why *do* my people war and fight,
when they've been told
about what's right?
They don't seem sorry for their ways
nor *want* to change to better days."

God thought awhile and then declared:
"The only one that can be spared
is Noah, who, it's plain to see,
has lived in peace, with his sons three.

"But every other living thing
will be destroyed by covering
the whole, wide world
with floods so great
I'll sweep away
the fear and hate."

To save him from the floods to come,
God spoke to Noah near his home.
An ark he must start building now,
four hundred feet from stern to prow,
three stories high, and extra wide,
with door and window on the side.

"It must be big, since in this boat
you'll need to keep yourself afloat —
your wife and sons and wives; then bring
a pair of every living thing
that creeps or crawls or runs or flies.
What space you'll need just for supplies!"

Shem, Japheth, Ham, the grown sons, three,
found each was willing to agree

and started building this great ark,
all working hard from dawn till dark.

They heard their neighbors
laugh and jeer
and say, "What crazy folks, and queer —
to build a boat on high, dry land!"
They just refused to understand.

The ark took many years to build.
God watched and waited
till they filled

the ship with all the needed things
for months of water voyaging.

Much food and clothing,
pots and plants
were stowed aboard.
They took no chance
of starving either beasts or men
while on the ark for weeks on end.

Next, Noah's search was not in vain:
from mountain, jungle, hill, and plain
he led the creatures two by two,
the tigers, bears, and kangaroo,
the horses, goats, and porcupines,
all trailing in in two long lines.

The sky was dark
with flapping wings;
the ground was 'live
with creeping things;

earth trembled at the mighty roar
of beasts all moving
toward the door.

Then Noah's wife and sons and wives
went up the ramp. They dried their eyes.
And as the sun shone hot about,
they heard the people laugh and shout.

Aboard at last! The rains did come;

they beat the roof with steady drum
for forty days and forty nights
as bit by bit land sank from sight.

The tops of mountains disappeared
as Noah from his windows peered.
An awesome sight, to look around
and see no trace of your home ground!

Can you imagine how you'd feel
to hear the thunder's crashing peal,
and pitch
    and toss
        in wind and storm —
the *only* ones alive and warm?

For six long months
on board they stayed.
It was not easy, but they prayed
that God would see them safely through
until dry land
came back in view.

The rains did stop; the flood went down
until the ark bumped on the crown
of mountain tall called Ararat,
and there the ship stuck fast, just sat.

Soon Noah let a raven go,
a big, black bird, which to and fro
went flying, finding food afloat
as they all watched it from the boat.

God sent strong winds the earth to dry,
yet still the waters seemed so high!
A dove flew next to look around
but did not find unflooded ground.

A week went by, and out again
this time the dove — oh, joy, amen! —
brought back a fresh-plucked olive leaf,
a sign of life! Oh, what relief!

Another week, the dove once more
was sent abroad to search, explore.
This time she did not reappear,
which meant that dry land
must be near.

The earth was drying rapidly,
and soon they found that they were free
to leave the ark. This happy throng
burst into sounds of joy and song.

To show their thanks
that they were spared,
the people built an altar there.
And God was pleased as He looked on;
He blessed good Noah and his sons.

To them He said, "Go build new homes;
have children who in turn will roam
and settle countries far and near.
Another flood you need not fear.

"To show you that My promise will
be kept forever, see that hill?
Beyond it I have placed up high
a lovely rainbow in the sky.

"By this fair sign will people know
My promise will be kept. So go
with faith to plant the earth again."
To this old Noah said,
"Amen!"

Dear Parents:

The world God made enjoyed peace with God, and there was harmony between creatures. But soon things became different. The Bible tells us that when God saw the violence on the earth, He decided to blot out both man and beast; He was sorry that He had made them. (Gen. 6:6, 7, 11-13)

But God decided to save Noah, a blameless man who walked with God, and through him give another chance to His creatures. So the story of God's judging the earth becomes the story of His saving it.

Christians have always seen Noah's ark as a picture of the salvation in Christ offered to us in Baptism (1 Peter 3:20, 21) and in the life of the Christian church, pictured as a ship on the stormy seas.

Will you help your child see the real meaning of the story? This is a story of God's caring and of His saving His creatures from the destruction that disobedience brings.

Whenever your child sees it raining, he should remember the promise God gave with the rainbow.

THE EDITOR